Corporate Governance

Concepts and Applications

Era of Modern Management
HR. Sustainable Development

Ibrahim H. Hussney
Accredited Lecturer and Instructor

© INTELLECTUAL PROPERTY RIGHTS

All rights reserved to the author, and this book may not be exchanged in whole or in part illegally; whether by making it available for downloading on websites or exchanging it via e-mail messages, no part of the text may be copied without its prior permission.

"Investing in building human beings is now at the top of the pyramid of states' concerns as the most important industry in this information age, as a result of nations realizing that their fate and future will always depend on the creativity of their citizens, and the extent of their challenge and response towards change always for the better....!!!!"

CONTENTS

Introduction ... Corporate Governance _____ 1

Chapter one ... Reasons for applying governance in organizations _____ 5

Chapter two ... The basic elements of governance in organizations _____ 14

Chapter Three ... Governance facing financial and accounting corruption _____ 30

Chapter four ... Tracks of governance classification in economic entities _____ 35

Chapter five ... Modern concepts of governance and management of economic entities _____ 39

Chapter six ... Governance and the role of state governments and legislative and oversight institutions _____ 45

Chapter seven ... Committees emanating from the Board of Directors _____ 59

Chapter eight ... Elements of the control environment in economic entities _____ 69

Chapter nine ... The general assembly of shareholders in economic entities _____ 78

Chapter ten ... Rules and methods of applying governance in economic entities _____ 82

Chapter eleven ... Governance policies and regulations in economic entities _____ 97

References_____ 104

INTRODUCTION ...
CORPORATE GOVERNANCE

The importance of governance has emerged during the past few decades when successive global financial crises have decimated the economies of a large number of developed countries and other emerging economies, but despite that, the concept of governance is still somewhat vague to many people.

Since the late 1970s, of the last century, the governance of economic entities, such as companies, has been the subject of great controversy and debate around the world, and in particular in the United States.

Taking into account the needs and desires of shareholders towards exercising their rights in the ownership of companies, and increasing the value of their shares.

The duties and responsibilities of the heads and directors of various companies have also expanded, and the duty of loyalty to these companies that they preside over and also to their shareholders has expanded.

In 1997, the Asian financial crisis affected the economies of many countries, such as Thailand, Indonesia, South Korea, Malaysia, and the Philippines, as it was affected by the exit of foreign capital after the collapse of property assets, and one of the most prominent weaknesses in these countries was the lack of mechanisms for the government to organize businesses management, and companies.

In the early 2000s, the massive bankruptcies resulting from the criminal offenses of Enron and WorldCom, as well as the failure of several other companies, such as Adelphia Communications, America Online, Arthur Andersen, Global Crossing, and Tyco, this failure reinforcing controls related to shareholder rights and interest corporate governance to manage it properly away from risks.

This reinforcement was reflected in the passage of the Sarbanes-Oxley Act of 2002, which is a US law that requires companies to ensure and approve financial information through internal control systems, and according to this law, the CEO and CFO will be held personally responsible for announcing any wrong financial statements. This law came as a result of the repercussions of the serious financial irregularities that led to the collapse of Enron and WorldCom.

There have been many opinions among different writers and researchers in expressing the concept or definition of the governance of organizations, business establishments, and companies, due to the multiplicity of interests and specializations of these writers and researchers.

Some have defined corporate governance as *a set of contractual relations that link the management of companies, shareholders, and stakeholders in them, through the procedures and methods used to manage the company's affairs and direct its business to ensure the development of performance and disclosure, transparency and*

Introduction

accountability, maximizing the benefit of shareholders in the long term, and taking into account the interests of the various parties.

Others have defined it by saying that *the concept of governance emphasizes the implementation of the principles of transparency, control, and financial and administrative accountability within organizations, business establishments, and companies, in a way that protects them from reaching the fate of collapsed companies.*

The comprehensiveness of the concept of governance of organizations, business establishments, and companies in many dimensions, whether economic, legal, administrative, accounting, social, or ethical, led to disagreement on finding a unified definition or concept of the term governance.

That the widespread of the concept of governance after the occurrence of many economic collapses and crises for many giant economic entities, has become an unequivocal indication of the effectiveness of the role played by this term and the means it includes for the treatment and reform of such collapses and crises.

Thus, the concept of governance must help eliminate conflict and achieve harmony and balance between the interests of the different groups that have an interest in economic entities, whether from within or from outside, by limiting management control and giving more powers to other groups, especially shareholders and other stakeholders.

The common denominator between the different concepts of the term governance indicates interest in developing performance and localizing the principles of disclosure, transparency, discipline, and justice within economic entities, which has been confirmed by many studies.

CHAPTER ONE ...
REASONS FOR APPLYING GOVERNANCE IN ORGANIZATIONS

Why is the business community around the world calling today for governance?

International interest in good governance has increased due to the exacerbation of the phenomenon of corruption and the problems resulting from it and to the growing negative economic and social effects of this corruption on development, especially in countries with emerging economies worldwide.

Many institutions and international non-governmental organizations have taken care of the issue of good governance, such as the World Bank, Transparency International, and other related organizations, as they have set standards related to it, and they are approved by their countries and institutions.

One of the most important factors that led to the reference to good governance is the exacerbation of the phenomenon of bribery, which is considered one of the most important manifestations of corruption, and one of the most serious crimes committed by public employees, which carries negative effects that are reflected on them in terms of compromising their integrity and the trust entrusted to them.

Organizational motives towards resorting to governance in organizations

Many organizational motives are leading to resorting to the application of governance in organizations, business establishments, and companies may be because risk management is ineffective, because internal control is weak, because managing the profits of the organization is going badly, or because negative behaviors are widespread from the top of the organizational hierarchy to the bottom. Or because there is a continuous failure in accounting and issuing reports for the organization or because there is a lack of proper practice in oversight, supervision, accountability, and transparency of transactions within the organization, business establishment, or company.

Objectives of resorting to governance in organizations

Just as there are organizational motives towards resorting to the application of governance, there are also goals envisaged in resorting to this approach, as the priority of these goals comes to the process of eliminating financial and administrative corruption in organizations, and strengthening affiliation to the organization, business institution, or company, and working on absenting the special agendas of some within the work environment, working to renounce the existence of paralysis, factionalism, and groups that resist the policies of change, and working to motivate the talents and energies of all employees in

Reasons for applying governance in organizations

organizations, business institutions, and companies, to exert the biggest effort they can.

Concept and definition of corporate governance

Governance is the set of processes, customs, laws, practices, policies, and regulations that influence the way an organization is managed, directed, or controlled.

Governance links the expectations of stakeholders with the goals of the organization that operates to achieve them. Governance is a system that ensures the activation of checks and balances between the Board of Directors, investors, and the various departments of the organization, to create an economic entity that works efficiently and is ideally directed, to enjoy long-term value.

Governance also works to meet the needs of shareholders and other stakeholders by directing and controlling the activities of management through the provision of good work, objectivity, accountability, and integrity.

It should be noted that sound governance depends on each of the commitment to the external market of the organization, business enterprise, or company, the legislation of the society in which these economic entities are located, as well as the culture of the board that protects each of the interests, policies, operations, and values... etc.

Advantages of applying governance in organizations

The first of these advantages is improving the financial performance of the organization, through elevating profits, increasing the return on investment, raising the value of shares, working to improve the means of cash flow, and improving the performance of the various operations in the organization, through building better operations systems and improving the quality of products and services, raise the efficiency of performance in all sectors, and enhance the organization's competitive advantage in the markets, by increasing the share of the product or service in the market.

Also, reducing the costs of marketing operations, and improving the organization's reputation in the business community, by increasing the demand for purchasing products, services, or shares, encouraging the demand for workers with these economic entities, and increasing opportunities for growth and expansion by increasing the market share, the availability of liquidity, and the emergence of good relations with banks and various financing institutions.

Among the advantages of applying governance in organizations are reducing the cost of capital for the organization by improving the financial results achieved for the organization, working to reduce costs, raising the competitive advantage of the organization in the markets, and improving the quality of workers in the organization through the rate of job turnover at a minimum.

Reasons for applying governance in organizations

Also, attracting competencies, providing systems for human resource development, increasing access to finance for the organization through increased cooperation with banks, improving the organization's ability to expand, and investing towards developing new products or services.

Governance is a safety factor when the heads of organizations resign or transfer ownership

The Board of Directors shall directly supervise the conduct of the company's business during the transitional period and work to appoint a new chairman. The Board of Directors also gives an institutional character that guarantees continuity after the transfer of ownership of the organization.

General concepts of good governance and its relationship to leadership in organizations

As we mentioned previously, governance is a system of oversight and guidance at the institutional level. It defines responsibilities, rights, and relationships with all concerned groups. It clarifies the rules and procedures necessary for rational decision-making related to the work of the organization. It serves as a system that supports justice, transparency, and institutional accountability, and enhances trust and credibility in the work environment.

Governance relates to leadership in organizations, business institutions, and companies, to ensure that they are managed and conduct their business effectively and properly, and to ensure that the systems and processes concerned are properly directed and ensure effective oversight and accountability.

Governance was defined by former World Bank President James David Wolfensohn as practices that revolve around justice, transparency, and accountability of officials, and the United Nations Development Program (UNDP) defined it as a system of laws and procedures that regulate the work of the social, political and economic sectors from two sides, in that, it establishes the system for their actions, and at the same time works to give them orders.

Good governance seeks to raise the efficiency of the performance of organizations, business establishments, and companies, and establish systems that ensure the elimination of unacceptable behavior by designing ways to control the performance of these economic entities.

Good governance framework, controls and determinants

External controls and determinants

External controls and determinants are responsible for controlling the general climate for investment in the country, which includes laws regulating economic activity such as money market and corporate laws, organizing competition, preventing monopolistic practices, bankruptcy, and combating corruption. It also includes the effectiveness and efficiency of oversight agencies and bodies in tightening control over all community organizations.

Reasons for applying governance in organizations

Internal controls and determinants

As for the internal controls and determinants, they are the ones that control the distribution of powers within the organization, business enterprise, or company, in the sense of controlling the state of the social climate within the organization, and the inter-relationships in the organization vertically and horizontally, between individuals and between different departments.

Good governance and anti-corruption in organizations

The phenomenon of corruption represents the most prominent problem facing development plans in all countries, especially countries with emerging economies (developing countries), and governance has come to resist and confront it.

Corruption has been defined by Transparency International as *"every act that involves the misuse of position or power to achieve a private interest, that is, to achieve a personal benefit for himself or his group."*

Reasons for financial and administrative corruption in organizations

Social reasons

Social unrest and anxiety resulting from the instability of the situation and fear of the upcoming unknown and collecting money by any means to face this unknown and mysterious future.

Corporate Governance

Economic reasons

The deteriorating economic conditions stimulate corruption behavior, as well as the high cost of living.

Administrative and organizational reasons

Complex procedures (bureaucracy), ambiguity and multiplicity of legislation or lack of action, as well as manifestations of impunity.

Manifestations of financial and administrative corruption in organizations

These manifestations are financial and administrative deviations, non-compliance with the rules and provisions that regulate the workflow in the organization, business enterprise, or company, and violation of the instructions of the regulatory bodies. Or carrying out actions other than what is stipulated in the organization's regulations or the principles of the profession.

The intervention of a person with "authority" in favor of those who do not deserve to be appointed or assuming a position, or referring an issue out of place … etc., and favoritism that refers to unjustly favoring one party over another, as is done in awarding bids, contracting, lease contracts, or investment projects, extortion and forgery that reflect the crime of obtaining money from people through job position under flimsy legal or administrative justifications, or concealing instructions in force on concerned people.

Reasons for applying governance in organizations

The effects of financial corruption on organizations, businesses, and public companies

Financial corruption will lead to a decrease in the efficiency of public investment and weaken the level of quality of public infrastructure, due to bribes that limit the resources allocated for investment and misdirect them or increase their cost. In addition, financial corruption weakens and may disrupt investment flows, thus contributing to low taxes and thus a decline in human development indicators, especially employment and health indicators.

Also among the effects is the deterioration of the fair distribution of wealth through the exploitation of influential people for their privileged positions in society, which allows them to monopolize the largest part of the economic benefits, in addition to their ability to accumulate assets continuously, which leads to widening the gap between this elite and the rest of the members of society.

CHAPTER TWO ...
BASIC ELEMENTS OF GOVERNANCE IN ORGANIZATIONS

The basic elements of governance in organizations, business enterprises, and companies focus on accountability, which is the ability to provide an explanation, justification, and acceptance of responsibility for actions and operations that took place in the organization, business enterprise, or company, and the role played by the official in the business and operations, and transparency, which is the principle of creating an environment in which information related to the circumstances, decisions, and actions of the organization, business enterprise, or company is available, visible, and understood.

Foundations and conditions of effective accountability

Accountability is not done randomly, but rather it is a planned, specific, known, and agreed-upon process, and therefore it must have basic foundations and requirements to achieve its effectiveness, and since accountability is a planned action and not randomly, great mental effort and interactive mental activity must be available.

Basic elements of governance in organizations

Accountability requires adult and responsible discipline from those involved, away from provoking any kind of tension, recklessness, or anger. Accountability must adhere to justice and preserve rights to advance the interest of the organization, business enterprise, or company, and to ensure that deviant behavior is not directed.

Types of accountability in organizations

Ethical accountability

Principles and practices of ethical accountability within an organization, business enterprise, or company aim to improve the normative behavior of both individuals and groups.

Administrative accountability

The employees of the organization, business enterprise, or company are subordinates within the hierarchy, and they are held accountable when any abuses occur while avoiding entering into any conflict of interest.

Accountability functions and the purpose of activating it in organizations

Activating the principle of accountability through governance, cannot be considered a source of threat in organizations, as much as it is a method for reviewing and improving performance and developing the skills of workers. Accountability supports resorting to strategic thinking at the level of individuals, groups, and departments, and it works to focus all the energies and resources available to the economic entities to maintain, support, and preserve their strategic objectives.

Accountability works to coordinate efforts at the level of individuals, groups, and departments, and to enhance forms of support and partnership among the working teams. It also works to detect gaps in performance at the level of individuals and departments in the organization and works to fix them, therefore it can be considered one of the important jobs.

Accountability works to strengthen the rational relations between the employer and the employees, by defining the obligations and duties of each party and providing the required support, in addition to presenting a clear picture of the expected results, which are required to be reached.

Motivations for accountability in organizations

External motivations

External motivations range from customer and consumer pressures, stakeholder pressures, civil society organizations pressures, and various media pressures.

Internal motivations

As for the internal motivations, they range from the pressures of internal control in the organizations, the pressures of the authorities for defining and distributing responsibilities, the organizational culture and professional ethics, and the pressures generated by colleagues in the profession.

Basic elements of governance in organizations

Obstacles to activating accountability in organizations

Administrative and structural obstacles

This type of obstacle includes weak comprehensive planning, complex regulations and procedures, centralization and weak decentralization, or weak protection for persons authorized to act.

Social and cultural obstacles

As for the social and cultural obstacles, they refer to the lack of training towards spreading the culture of accountability, the spread of corruption without activating the concept of accountability, the poor socialization of new workers, especially in the field of accountability, the dominance of loyalties and the prevalence of nepotism and favoritism in the work of the concerned administration.

The ultimate goal of activating the principle of accountability in organizations

The ultimate goal behind accountability is to know the responsible party and determine the type of responsibility and the nature of the behavior that is in violation of the regulations and may be illegal, and strive to preserve the rights of all employees of the organization, in the face of what may be issued by the management of arbitrariness, and enabling them to hold officials accountable in their various positions in the various departments.

Governance and the principle of transparency

Definition and concept

is the free flow of information in its broadest sense, that is, providing information and working in an open manner that allows stakeholders to obtain it to preserve their interests, make appropriate decisions, and discover errors to correct them.

Its concept indicates that it is the principle of creating an environment in which information related to circumstances, decisions, and actions in the organization is available, visible, and understood, i.e., providing information and making decisions known by declaring them promptly and making them available to all relevant parties.

The foundations required to activate the principle of transparency

The first foundation required to activate the principle of transparency in organizations is **the validity and credibility of information,** meaning the inevitability of clear procedures, validity, credibility, and clarity of the information presented and data related to administrative units, individuals, or groups within the organization, and the second foundation is what refers to **the right of access to information,** i.e. inevitability availability of the right that allows everyone involved in the matter to obtain and access the correct relevant information and the facts it reveals promptly.

Basic elements of governance in organizations

The importance of activating the principle of transparency

The importance of activating the principle of transparency in organizations lies in helping towards making correct administrative and financial decisions, providing means of success and continuity for any economic entity that wants to combat corruption in all its forms, facilitating the process of performance appraisal, saving time and effort, and avoiding chaos in business management. Consolidate the values of cooperation and teamwork in a team spirit, localize the principles of consultation and accountability and ensure their success, remove bureaucratic and routine obstacles, and help raise the level of trust between all departments, groups, and individuals.

Objectives of activating the principle of transparency

One of the objectives of activating the principle of transparency in organizations is to work to weaken the chances of corruption spreading in the economic entities, raise the level of awareness among subordinates regarding their rights and duties, and motivate them to participate and demand their needs.

Also among the objectives are making the most logical and objective decisions, reducing the phenomenon of moody decision-making, enhancing the institutional spirit within the organization, enhancing trust and raising the degree of loyalty to customers and consumers, as well as raising the quality of products and services provided, and improving the level of response to the needs and desires of customers and consumers, in addition to achieving financial discipline and controlling spending, reducing waste of public money while preserving assets, and working to reduce the costs of related projects.

Benefits of applying the principle of transparency

In general, the application of the principle of transparency in organizations will contribute to improving the levels of understanding of subordinates and stakeholders of business structures and activities, in addition to understanding the policies of these economic entities, their levels of performance regarding environmental and ethical standards, and the relationship of these entities with the communities in which they operate.

The principle of transparency works to consolidate the values of cooperation, coordination, and concerted efforts among individuals, work groups, and departments, which ultimately leads to obtaining objective and clear results, where work is performed collectively and in a team spirit, as well as collective accountability for violations.

Applying the principle of transparency to the administrative and financial operations of organizations will result in saving time, effort, and costs, avoiding confusion and chaos in presenting business, in addition to developing the functions of administrative units, from specialized administrative units to work teams that perform their tasks better and more transparency, given that the efforts made are joint efforts of all members of the administrative unit.

The application of the principle of transparency will work to change the prevailing organizational culture in organizations and this requires the localization of positive attitudes among subordinates that indicate that the most important thing in the existing entity is working to provide products and services of high quality to customers, consumers, and stakeholders, with the need to deal with them with a high level of transparency free from complications and routine.

The principle of transparency works to transform the criteria for promotion to the higher position that are based on the performance of the subordinate to depend on his ability and competence, that is, the need for their performance of their work to be clear and effective, and then work to reward them for these capabilities with promotions, which must be consistent with upgrading to a certain level of performance transparently, this encourages a spirit of competition among subordinates, which in turn leads to positive effects related to job performance.

Also, the application of the principle of transparency in organizations will help to adopt an educational policy aimed at increasing and improving the skills of subordinates instead of relying on the traditional training and education methods used, which works to expand the perceptions of subordinates more transparently and consolidate this in their minds.

The principle of transparency seeks to reduce centralization in the various economic entities by reducing the broad powers in decision-making processes and seeks to encourage the launch of initiatives to allow every good initiative to take its role in practical application and for subordinates in entities that adopt transparency to enjoy greater independence while carrying out their job duties, which enhances the activation of the issue of self-monitoring for them instead of continuous administrative control, which is reflected in making their work more transparent, credible and objective.

The principle of transparency allows the selection of administrative leaders with integrity, honesty, objectivity, affiliation, and loyalty to the entity and the public interest, and a deep understanding of the financial position of the entity, and all financial aspects related to individual and collective performance, and they are responsible to each other for the overall performance and achievement of the goals of the organization, and thus control becomes always activated by everyone and to everyone.

Requirements for applying the principle of transparency

There are many basic requirements that must be met to enhance the role of transparency, which has become a prerequisite for strengthening administrative and organizational processes if the organization wants to raise the level of the management of its implementation, therefore, let it be understood that the requirements for the success of integrity and transparency are multiple, and the most important of them is the need for administrative development in the management of these entities, and this development cannot be done separately from the development of human calibers, and the availability of

Basic elements of governance in organizations

continuous coordination between the various relevant departments, and linking training to the needs of the entity.

Objectively speaking the policy in selection and appointment should be based on the principle of competence, and the need to work on developing a wide network of information between the administrative units inside and outside the entity in order to provide a high degree of coordination, cooperation, and accuracy in procedures and work to strengthen the role of oversight because of its great impact towards enhancing transparency.

It is also required to resort to simplifying work procedures in a way that allows the performance of administrative and financial activities without underestimation or negligence and to review laws, regulations, and rules periodically in order to address ambiguous paragraphs and clarify them for subordinates and stakeholders and to evaluate institutional performance and the performance of subordinates and senior leadership in direct relation to the goals of transparency and fighting corruption, and work to develop evaluation mechanisms and criteria on a regular basis.

And the need to provide clear and specific communication channels and contact tools that enable subordinates to report the existence of cases of deviation easily and without exposure to long and complex procedures, and to adopt specific procedures to ensure the availability of integrity and accountability, and to include effective disciplinary procedures for subordinates in organizations, business establishments, or companies, with the aim of encouraging them to stay away from behaviors that bring them closer to administrative and financial deviations.

Focusing on improving the efficiency of administrative leaders through better training for subordinates and choosing the best of them, with evaluation and review of the nature of the work they practice within the entity with the aim of achieving job stability in the end and relying on the mechanism of rotating subordinates so that they do not stay in one place for a long time that enables them to build personal relationships and expose them external pressures may have a negative impact on achieving transparency.

Also among the requirements is spreading awareness and explaining the benefits of activating the principle of transparency by subordinates in various aspects of practice and family life, by adhering to ethical values that contribute to combating forms of corruption.

And work to develop the mechanisms of business supervision by works leaders and managers towards the allegations of subordinates and follow them up, and work on the distribution of roles in order to ensure the continuity of the functioning of the work wheel with the required clarity and ease, and in order to establish the rules of job stability.

Finally, working to motivate subordinates to announce any conflict of interest that may result in suspicion of financial or administrative corruption, by working to provide an incentive system that encourages subordinates to adhere to professional ethics, activate each of the principles of honesty and integrity, and adhere to work rules, its regulations, and systems with the aim of enhancing administrative and financial transparency.

Levels of application of the principle of transparency

There are two levels for applying transparency in organizations. The first level is called **the self-level of transparency,** which is the level that includes both legislation and laws, and transparency of procedures, which are procedures that are self-approved by the entity, for the purpose of monitoring and localizing the principle of transparency.

The second level is what is **called the comprehensive level of transparency,** which includes the procedures that are approved by the country in which the organization, business institution, or company operates, for the purpose of monitoring and localizing the principle of transparency in a comprehensive manner.

Mechanisms to achieve transparency of legislation and procedures

Mechanisms for achieving transparency of legislation and procedures in each of the organizations, business establishments, or companies include work to assess the performance of all subordinates in the organization on a regular and continuous basis and work to ensure that the selection and appointment of human resources are based on clear foundations and criteria and far from mediocrity, nepotism, and favoritism, and it is imperative for the entity relevant, announcing all applicable laws and regulations in a clear and integrated manner to all subordinates working there.

And work to clarify the rights, duties, and responsibilities of subordinates and provide clear mechanisms to identify them, and work to educate subordinates about the nature of the organization's tasks, and work to announce all cases that are characterized by creativity and distinction from subordinates, as well as cases of failure or abuse that occur, so that this serves as a mechanism To encourage on the one hand and deter on the other.

Mechanisms to achieve comprehensive transparency at the societal level of the state

These mechanisms include emphasizing the state's commitment and adherence to laws, developing and activating the role of oversight and accounting agencies, working to evaluate the performance of administrative leaders in all sectors regularly, working to establish a special center for preserving and exchanging information and data, documenting the state's legislation and laws related to all sectors in which it operates, and working on the availability of documents that include this information and data to be accessible to those who request it.

And resorting to holding meetings periodically and regularly between the central agencies concerned with administration and control in the country, to provide mechanisms for coordination and follow-up of control operations, to facilitate the work of these agencies, control matters related to violations, and combat all forms of corruption and deviations.

Basic elements of governance in organizations

Policies and procedures to be taken into account when applying transparency

It is necessary to resort to using the method of issuing instructions that are directed to subordinates related to work policies and procedures, about amendments, changes, cancellations, and suspensions that occur in laws, regulations, and regulations, and the need to educate subordinates and increase their knowledge of the administrative and organizational dimensions within the organization, business enterprise, or company, and to familiarize them with their rights, duties, and responsibilities, to give them a clear picture of the goals and activities of the different administrative levels.

Also, the need to work on preparing and printing manuals for the regulations, laws, and instructions related to the work programs and the entity's employees, so that they become a reference that can be referred to define duties and responsibilities, preserve rights and workflow, and to become more clear between subordinates and the entity.

Mechanisms for measuring the level of transparency

Transparency came to eliminate corruption, or at least to limit its destructive impact on business, so measuring the level of corruption is inversely proportional to measuring the level of transparency, and this matter represents a very important issue and requires a careful system to verify the validity of the results of this measurement, and also comes to understand the nature of the phenomenon of corruption and the factors that cause it and the relative weight of these factors, and the differentiation between the different natures of corruption such as bribery, abuse of influence, nepotism, waste of public money…etc.

Corruption is difficult to control simply and determine its size, but the higher the level of integrity and administrative accountability in organizations, business institutions, and companies, and in the presence of effective transparency, the more there is the ability to confront and limit corruption.

Also, always work through serious investigation and other mechanisms to identify the situation, to obtain statistics on the extent of corruption in the relevant entity, with constant emphasis that the data of these available statistics are approximate and not real.

Also, work on classifying the approximate statistics data that were reached and attributing them to the type of corruption from which they were derived, such as bribery, abuse of influence, nepotism, or waste of public money…etc., and thus we can obtain data for comparative statistics, and this can be reached based on specific criteria, foundations and measurements such as heritage, culture, educational level, belief, and the experiences of other countries…etc.

It is very important to identify the degree of penetration of corruption in the various administrative levels in organizations, business establishments, and companies, that is, in their internal environment, and also not to overlook the effects of corruption that may result from the external environment, while working to determine the indirect cost of corruption, as the direct cost is In funds

Basic elements of governance in organizations

and resources, while the indirect effects are represented in the effects that can occur and affect the quality of the product, the cost of services, and also affect the general level of the state, such as the deficit in the public budget arising from the deficit in the balance of payments, and other negative effects on savings, investment, public debt...etc.

CHAPTER THREE ... GOVERNANCE FACING FINANCIAL AND ACCOUNTING CORRUPTION

The source of the financial crises to which many economic entities around the world are exposed is mainly considered as arising from many cases of corruption, especially financial and accounting corruption, which leaves a negative impact in many areas, as it becomes one of the most prominent economic fields, and the most important effect of that is the incurring of a campaign stocks result in heavy financial losses that negatively affect the credibility of organizations, business establishments, and companies that are invested in, and on the capital markets through the tendency of current and prospective investors to search for alternative investment outlets. This important matter prompted the relevant authorities at the national and international levels to conduct studies to identify the main reasons behind the occurrence of financial crises and propose ways to protect the rights of shareholders and other stakeholders.

General rules for combating financial and accounting corruption

One of the general rules for confronting financial and accounting corruption in organizations, business establishments, and companies is to adopt and activate the principles of transparency and disclosure of financial and non-financial information, and to adopt a set of high-level accounting standards that are consistent with the interests of shareholders and other stakeholders, and to enhance the shareholder's vulnerability, and stakeholders to make the right economic decisions regarding the future of their investments and the continuation of their activities in the organizations, and to adopt and activate a governance framework based on a specific set of general principles, and aims to protect the rights of shareholders and other stakeholders.

Organizations most affected by financial and accounting corruption

Joint-stock companies are considered among the business institutions most affected by financial and accounting corruption, as a result of the spread of several negative factors, such as the lack of clarity in the frameworks and controls of the responsibilities of the Board of Directors and senior executives, the absence of transparent financial reports and the failure to follow high-quality standards in the field of accounting measurement and disclosure, the absence of a clear definition of the rights of shareholders in joint stock companies and the rights of other stakeholders.

Also, among the negative factors leading to this damage is the low circulation of information, the absence of support for the independence of auditors, the failure to enhance the level of consistency of accounting treatments required according to the unified accounting system with international accounting standards, and the lack of public awareness of the importance of resorting to governance to confront cases of corruption, and identifying the importance of governance towards facing future challenges in many areas in the era of globalization, and the shortcomings of the legal and regulatory frameworks that regulate the work of this type of companies, as well as what is related to establishing general principles of governance.

The direct causes of financial crises and collapse of organizations

These reasons vary between manipulation of financial reports and failure to disclose the facts of the prevailing conditions, and by working to inflate the annual profits of companies, amending audited financial reports, submitting amended copies to the trading commission in the stock market, and raising doubts about the credibility of accounting firms, and audit, and the eligibility of its members and the adequacy of professional standards (accounting and auditing) and the level of commitment to apply them.

Also, not to disclose the results of the work of the special units of the organizations, business establishments, or companies (which are managed by employees who receive large rewards for that), and which are carried out separately from the results of the work of those companies, and not to disclose also the future contracts of the related financial derivatives the entity's activities or appropriate treatment, as well as non-disclosure of extra-budgetary financing activities that include unannounced claims by organizations, business establishments, or companies.

Governance facing financial and accounting corruption

Anoplasty management of the affairs of entities, and the lack of standards that govern the behavior of workers

This angioplasty arises as a result of loyalty that is not directed to the right place and people, by giving confidence to people who are not entrusted with their duties within the economic entities, towards shareholders, stakeholders, and towards obedience to laws and regulations. Also, many managers in the various entities do not have sufficient capacity to exercise their duties and assume their professional responsibilities, because they only assume their positions through their appointment in ways that do not amount to verifying the required professional role that must be exercised by those managers.

In addition to that, the failure of the boards of directors and their affiliated committees in the various entities towards assuming the responsibilities entrusted to them and bypassing the clear warning signs of the imminent occurrence of the crisis, as well as the weakness of the control and supervision systems, and the misuse of the systems for determining the rewards of executive subordinates and motivating them.

It cannot be overlooked the low levels of trust in the leaders of major entities, as a result of the lack of transparency and non-dissemination of financial and non-financial information, which affects the boards of directors, executive departments, and auditors in companies, which also leads to asserting that the problem is lack of integrity, as well as incompetence management and weak supervision compared to the problems arising from the fluctuations of financial markets.

The financial, economic, and social effects of widespread corruption in various entities

The financial and economic effects of rampant corruption in the various economic entities reflected by organizations, business establishments, and companies range from a decrease in the market prices of these entities' shares in the financial stock exchanges, the loss of workers' jobs, the loss of their rights in savings funds, and a decrease in the general level of confidence in the accounting and auditing profession and the quality of the criteria on which it is based, and the severe financial losses that cause damage to the interests of shareholders and other stakeholders.

Governance work determinants in economic entities

Governance work determinants in economic entities are based on both **guidance and control** through the system by which these entities are directed and controlled, and on the **participating parties** by identifying those parties related to governance and clarifying the duties, responsibilities, and powers granted to them according to specific concepts, and on the added value, from by identifying its source as a value-added to shareholders and other stakeholders.

CHAPTER FOUR ...
TRACKS OF GOVERNANCE CLASSIFICATION IN ECONOMIC ENTITIES

Track of directing and controlling performance

This track focuses on the relationship of governance to direction and control performance in organizations, the easiest and most common definition in this field is provided by the Cadbury Committee, which is stipulated in its report issued in 1992, in Britain on the financial aspects of corporates, where it was defined as *"the system by which companies direct and control"*.

The track of identifying parties related to governance

Through this track, the duties, responsibilities, and powers granted to employees of organizations, business establishments, and companies related to corporate governance are clarified according to clear and specific concepts, and thus governance is accordingly the way through which the Board of Directors, managers, as well as auditors can assume their responsibilities in all fairness and transparency, and face the questions and inquiries of shareholders and other stakeholders in this regard.

Corporate Governance

The track of governance objectives and their importance

Through this track, the focus is placed on the objectives of governance and its importance to shareholders and other stakeholders, and it is considered as a source of value for shareholders within its limited scope and a source of value for other stakeholders in the organization, within the broader scope of governance.

Different objectives according to governance models

The objectives of corporate governance vary according to the models of governance themselves, which in reality reflect the implicit objectives of corporate activities and the diversity of parties associated with them in various countries of the world.

Governance aims to encourage boards of directors to control and supervise the various departments to enhance the welfare of the economy of the entities, including the welfare of shareholders, employees, and the welfare of society.

Governance and its economic importance

The quality of governance, and the ability to understand the rights of shareholders, are considered as important control systems for the success of investments in various economic entities.

Tracks of governance classification in economic entities

Governance and the degree of the economic performance of the entity, work to provide an appropriate amount of reassurance to current shareholders and prospective investors, to achieve an appropriate return on their investments while maximizing the value of shareholders and preserving their rights, especially the small number of shareholders.

The fact indicates that economic entities that enjoy good governance must have managers who enjoy high levels of quality, and these entities deal more transparently, which enhances confidence among shareholders and stakeholders, and this transparency works to reduce investment risks, and thus reduce capital costs.

The adoption of good governance standards will certainly have a direct impact on the financial markets, as the application of these standards will enhance the efficiency of the markets, and provide appropriate information for investors to learn more about the performance of organizations, business institutions, and various companies, and realize the level of implementation of strategies for these entities, and methods of identifying risks, as well as ways to manage them.

We must emphasize that there is a close link between governance and the economic system of the state because the problems resulting from the weak governance of the various economic entities are not only caused by the failure of investments, but the reasons extend to become represented in weak levels of public confidence in all businesses, or other words Loss of credibility for the entire economic system, and therefore the improvement of governance must be seen as a gain for all relevant parties, that is, for those entities and shareholders, and a gain for the national economy through the stable, continuous and more efficient activity of these entities operating under its umbrella.

Governance and its legal importance

Laws and regulations are considered safety valve that ensures the application of good governance, so the standards of disclosure, transparency, and standards of accounting and auditing systems must form the backbone of the principles of successful corporate governance.

Auditing standards are considered the backbone of the governance framework, as these laws and standards regulate the relationship between the parties related to the entity, as well as those concerned with the national economy of the state.

The different types of contracts between all concerned parties in the economic entity, whatever its type, represent the cornerstone for regulating the contractual relations between them in a way that guarantees the rights of each of these parties, and despite that we have to understand that it can result from irresponsible practices that violate the formulas of these contracts concluded or the laws, decisions, and basic systems regulating the economic entity.

CHAPTER FIVE ...
MODERN CONCEPTS OF GOVERNANCE AND MANAGEMENT OF ECONOMIC ENTITIES

Governance and the role of the board of directors

The Board of Directors of various economic entities, such as organizations, business establishments, and companies, has full powers, and at the same time, it has to assume all responsibilities.

As the positive impact of governance on the management of these entities is represented in giving priority to the strengthening of public interest, which is reflected in the strengthening of the economy from the concept that sound management of organizations, business institutions, and companies is management not only for economic development but also for social development.

The board and its subcommittees represent a complete and unspecified means of communication with officials and employees, as they have the freedom to seek the assistance of consultants for purposes, they deem important.

Corporate Governance

The board usually requests the submission of suggestions by its members, committees, and employees who occupy the upper levels, in a way that provides a positive and effective atmosphere that enables it to manage the economic entity within clear bases in terms of fiduciary responsibility, transparency, accountability and control within the required ethical environment.

Companies in the United States of America have become completely subject to the Board of Directors, which can choose the CEO of the company and give him broad powers to manage the daily work wheel, with the continued need to obtain the approval of the members of the board to take actions of utmost importance, such as mergers, investment, and major capital expansions. , or others, such as entering into high-cost projects, and the board's tasks remained related to formulating and setting policies, making decisions, monitoring the performance of various departments, determining, controlling, and oversight.

Governance and the separation of management from ownership

The separation of management from ownership and control of administrative decisions away from shareholders necessitated the existence of a system of controls, as the parties involved in managing companies include, in addition to the Board of Directors, the CEO, that is, the general manager, the executive departments of the organization, and the employees, and thus all those involved in the management of the company, whether directly or indirectly, they became stakeholders.

Modern concepts of governance and management of economic entities

Governance and management models of economic entities

There are many different models for managing economic entities around the world, and they differ from one model to another according to the approved economic vision.

The liberal management model of governance encourages innovation and competition in terms of quality and cost, and we will find it common in Anglo-American countries, where it tends to give priority to the interests of shareholders, while the harmonized model of governance facilitates innovation and increased competition in quality, and these models can find in common in European countries and Japan, and this model focuses on the interests of workers, managers, suppliers, customers, and society as a whole, thus, we can confirm that each kind of these models has a competitive advantage that distinguishes it from others.

References for governance controls in economic entities

Governance mechanisms and controls aim to reduce deficiencies that arise from abuses and ethical risks, and to monitor the behavior of workers and managers in organizations, business establishments, and companies, as an independent third party monitors the accuracy of information provided by management to investors, and to reach this, compliance is considered the internal control system serves as the main reference for defining these controls, and these references can be summarized in the

Board of Directors, internal control, the balance of power, and accounting discipline.

Controls of the board of directors in economic entities

The Board of Directors has the necessary powers to manage the economic entity that is provided to it by law, and it is the body capable of monitoring the performance of executive managers for their work and providing the necessary guarantees to investors to protect their capital.

Internal controls in economic entities

Ensuring the existence of internal control that is practiced within specific controls through regulations and instructions, which are carried out by internal and external audits, ensures reasonable guarantees to the economic entity to achieve its objectives and protect it from risks, it also gives confidence in adherence to instructions and laws, which increases confidence in financial and operational reports.

Controls of the balance of power in the economic entities

In 2001, after the collapse of many major American companies such as Enron and WorldCom, the US government passed the so-called Sarbanes-Oxley Act, to restore confidence in the management of American companies, and to create a balance of power, especially between management and corporate performance oversight bodies.

The forces that directly control companies, represented by the Board of Directors, regulatory authorities, external oversight, and the business community, have been identified.

While the forces that indirectly control companies are competitors, creditors, speculators in financial markets, shareholders, and various events.

Accounting discipline controls in economic entities

The term creative accounting is applied to those works that aim to beautify the results of economic entities in a manner that is not consistent with their real results, which may lead to the collapse of those entities, due to the contribution of this type of accounting to showing these lists untrue in line with the desire of departments in these entities, not taking into account the interest of the beneficiaries of the shareholders.

The objectives of resorting to creative accounting

One of the most important goals of resorting to what is called creative accounting is tax manipulation, achieving personal interests, obtaining professional classifications, influencing the price of shares in financial markets, facilitating the process of borrowing from financial institutions, or positively affecting the company's reputation in the market.

Here we must point out that governance plays a major role in reducing the effects of negative creative accounting, by emphasizing the role of auditors and work ethics and focusing on the legal responsibilities of all parties to prevent the exploitation of some loopholes in the law, or to provide a misleading presentation about profits.

For example, this may be linked to future expectations or part of it is postponed from good years to other years to come, or modification and change in accounting policies and estimates to achieve certain goals.

CHAPTER SIX ...
GOVERNANCE AND THE ROLE OF STATE GOVERNMENTS AND LEGISLATIVE AND OVERSIGHT INSTITUTIONS

It is the responsibility of the governments of different countries around the world. Their legislative and oversight institutions play the main role in activating the precise direction to develop the legislative system for the governance of the economic entities in which it operates, in a way that allows the application of all rules related to governance, as well as to support the promotion and awareness raising processes related to its culture and applications.

Where all this comes to consolidate the thought of governance and increase the rates of transparency and disclosure, reduce corruption, and adopt fair treatment for all investors.

Governance and developing the investment climate and increasing economic growth

The governance of economic entities is characterized by the applicability to achieve many advantages, such as reducing the impact of risks and crises, providing financing and reducing the cost of capital, improving operating efficiency and supporting performance oversight, achieving the best possible sustainability rates for organizations, business institutions, and companies, and helping so-called family companies to transform into an institutional form and avoid conflicts of interest in the dealings of related parties with each other.

Governance also plays a pivotal role in protecting the rights of shareholders and owners of money, the rights of its employees, and the rights of those dealing with the economic entity and state agencies, and the effects of governance also extend to protect society as a whole and the environment in which the economic entity operates.

A-Scope vocabularies that covered by governance process in countries

Without prejudice to all legislation and regulatory regulations regulating the work of all economic entities within the country, the rules related to governance apply to all listed and non-listed companies in the stock market, various financing institutions, banking and non-banking institutions, and industrial, commercial and service companies, regardless of their size and nature of the activity, whether they are family businesses or publicly owned.

It should not be understood that the application of governance is only a commitment to a set of rules that must be adopted and acted upon, but rather it is considered as a culture and a method towards controlling the relationship between the owners of money, its Board of Directors, and those dealing with the economic entity, which reflects advantages and benefits on it and the whole society.

Governance and the role of state governments and legislative and oversight institutions

Compulsory disclosure and adoption of the rule of compliance and interpretation when not applied

In a manner that does not contradict the provisions of laws, legislations, and regulatory regulations of countries, the principle is that economic entities work to implement all the rules of governance approved in the country, and when they are unable to apply some of these rules for any reason, these entities must make disclosures and interpret that in an objective and acceptable manner, in front of the authorities related to the application of the rules of governance, under the rule of compliance and interpretation, each entity must provide evidence of the rules it will adhere to and what it has not currently complied with justifications for non-compliance, and also provide what is related to its plans for full implementation.

Principles of general references globally for the preparation of governance rules

Availability of a general framework for the application of governance

The need to ensure that the state has a general and effective framework for applying the rules of governance, that the framework guarantees the efficiency and transparency of markets and compliance with legislation and laws, and that it stipulates the need to define responsibilities between the various legislative and supervisory authorities.

Corporate Governance

Ensuring rights and equal treatment for shareholders

The corporate governance framework must guarantee protection for all shareholder's rights and equal treatment among them, especially small and foreign shareholders and all shareholders should have the opportunity to obtain actual compensation in case their rights are violated.

The role of investors and dealers in financial markets

The general framework of governance in the country must provide economic incentives for investors and dealers in financial markets during the investment cycle to ensure the efficient management of these markets and ensure the optimal application of governance.

The role of stakeholders

The governance framework in countries must include recognition of stakeholders' rights as stipulated in laws, and the framework should also work to encourage cooperation between different economic entities and stakeholders, to maximize wealth, create job opportunities, and achieve sustainability for projects based on sound financial foundations.

Governance and the role of state governments and legislative and oversight institutions

Principles of disclosure and transparency

The governance framework in countries should ensure the principle of accurate and timely disclosure of important matters that result in material events, related to economic entities, their financial position, performance, and ownership structure, as well as the method of exercising management in them.

The role and responsibilities of the board of directors

The governance framework in the countries must provide strategic guidelines for guiding the economic entities, and it must also ensure the effective follow-up of the executive management by the Board of Directors and ensure the accountability of the board by the company and the shareholders.

Vocabularies for applying good governance in economic entities

Board of directors

In a manner that does not contradict the law and the articles of association of each of the various economic entities, such as organizations, business establishments, and companies, the Board of Directors shall be formed from an appropriate number of members in a manner that enables it to carry out its functions and duties.

Corporate Governance

The majority of the Board members must be independent and non-executive, and it must include at least two independent members with great technical and analytical skills, and selection and appointment must be based on international standards without prejudice to a particular gender, creed, color, etc.

In all cases, when selecting the independent and non-executive members, consideration must be taken that the member can allocate sufficient time and attention to the entity and that there is no conflict with his other interests.

Basic requirements for the board of directors to perform its duties

The secretary of the board plays the role of the link between the members and each other and between the Board of Directors and the senior management of the economic entity, and he works to provide sufficient information, and data, about the entity to the new members of the Board of Directors upon their appointment, so that they can be familiar with all the general aspects of this entity, and touch the strengths and sources of Its weaknesses, its administrative structure, and its budget components.

The Board of Directors elects the Chairman of the Board and appoints the Managing Director, and it is not preferable to combine the positions of Chairman and Managing Director, and if this is not possible, and based on international standards, an independent deputy chairman of the Board of Directors is appointed, as he presides over meetings that discuss the performance of the entity's executive departments.

Governance and the role of state governments and legislative and oversight institutions

Board meeting determinants

The Board of Directors must convene at least once every three months, with the possibility of the board seeking help from whomever it sees from inside or outside the entity to discuss some issues related to it, provided that disclosure is made in the annual report and the report of the Board of Directors on the number of meetings and the names of the members who were absent from attending the meetings of the board or the meetings of its committees.

It is taken into account that the member should not be absent from more than one-third of the number of board meetings in a year and that the meetings are called for at times, places, and according to arrangements that facilitate the members' attendance.

The Board of Directors may resort to modern visual and audio means of communication to hold its meetings, provided that the articles of the association of the economic entity stipulate this, and the board sets controls for the use of these means regarding holding meetings and remote participation of members.

Role of the board of directors in the economic entity

The Board of Directors of the economic entity plays an important and decisive role in setting strategic goals, approving general plans and policies related to the work wheel, monitoring the performance of executive departments, ensuring the effectiveness of the internal control and risk management system, determining the optimal method for applying governance, and adopting professional policies and standards that must be followed by employees, therefore, the decisions of the Board of Directors have a significant impact on the company's performance in a way that guarantees the preservation of its assets and the maximization of the wealth of its shareholders.

The Board of Directors assumes management based on a mandate from the General Assembly, and therefore the final responsibility rests with it, even if it forms committees, or delegates other entities or individuals to carry out some of its work, and the decisions of the board are issued by majority, and if the board is forced to take decisions by passing as a result of emergency circumstances, voting must take place with the participation of all members.

Duties and responsibilities of the Board of Directors

One of the tasks and responsibilities of the boards of directors in the various economic entities is that they develop training plans for the members of these boards, which include the thought and culture of governance, the work tasks of these boards and their committees, and any other issues that the boards deem important for their members.

Also, work to develop a scheme for the succession of power within the economic entity, for senior administrative positions, as well as members of the Board of Directors, in a way that guarantees the sustainability of the entity and the effective functioning of its business.

Governance and the role of state governments and legislative and oversight institutions

The Board of Directors must appoint a secretary with competence and understanding of all the business of the economic entity. The board can also establish an organizational unit for the secretariat according to the size and needs of the entity, and general supervision of the process of data disclosure and communication channels, ensuring the integrity of the financial and accounting reports issued by the entity, as well as ensure the independence of both the internal audit activity and compliance with the organization.

Among the responsibilities of the Board of Directors is to meet with the entity's managers to consult with them, whether in the presence or absence of the Executive Board members, provided that coordination takes place with them through the secretary of the Board of Directors towards setting appointments and informing them of what will be consulted about.

The board shall determine the powers that it delegates to one of its members, committees, or others. It must also specify the duration of the delegation, the periodicity of the reports it obtains from the committees and the executive management, and follow up on the results of the exercise of those delegated powers, the board can also request an external advisory opinion on any of the matters.

The entity, when approved by the majority of the members of the board, provided that the provisions for avoiding conflicts of interest are taken into account, and noted that the use of consultants does not relieve the members of the board from their responsibility.

The Board of Directors is responsible for putting in place preventive measures, tools, and mechanisms that secure the flow of information, control the accuracy and integrity of data within the economic entity, and protect it from manipulation or penetration, whether from inside or outside the entity, such as securing the use of the Internet and mobile devices against penetration and piracy.

The Board of Directors must set up mechanisms and systems that ensure the commitment of all employees of the entity to the laws, charters, and internal policies thereof, and it must also be responsible for setting up an early warning system to detect any defect or deviation that may occur within the entity and to ensure the speedy taking of appropriate measures, this system must include a way to protect information sources and whistleblowers of corruption and deviation.

Role and responsibilities of the Chairman of the Board of Directors

The chairman of the Board of Directors is responsible for the level of quality of the board's performance in general, and he is responsible for guiding and directing the board and ensuring the effectiveness of this performance, and ensuring the effectiveness of the governance system applied in the economic entity he heads, as well as the effectiveness of the performance of the board committees, as well as making sure that adequate and accurate information is made available promptly to board members and shareholders.

Also, the Chairman of the Board of Directors has to receive reports and recommendations from all committees and present them to the board regularly to take the necessary action in their regard, and to ensure that all

Governance and the role of state governments and legislative and oversight institutions

members of the board conduct a self-assessment that shows the extent of the member's commitment to the duties of his job, and to invite the ordinary and extraordinary general assembly to convene and to consider the agenda presented by board, encouraging debate and ensuring that dissenting opinions can be expressed and discussed within the framework of the decision-making process.

He must also ensure that the board is committed to accomplishing its tasks in the best way and interest of the organization, with the need to avoid conflict of interests, and he must also strive to maintain bonds of trust between all members of the board, especially between the executive and non-executive members, with the need to strengthen the relationship of the board as a whole with management and with the supreme authority of the economic entity and to ensure that decision-making takes place on a sound basis and a comprehensive knowledge of the issues, with the need to stress the existence of an appropriate mechanism to ensure the effective implementation of those decisions promptly.

Role and responsibilities of the Managing Director

Managing Director is the member at the top of executive management in the economic entity, as he must implement the entity's annual strategy and plan, which was formulated and approved by the Board of Directors, and he must work on implementing all internal policies, regulations, and systems and determine the terms of reference and responsibilities of all employees of the entity by the work regulations and decisions of the Board of Directors.

Corporate Governance

The managing director can suggest topics that can be raised in the periodic meetings of the board in consultation with the chairman of the board, actively participate in building and developing a culture of ethical values within the economic entity, and propose reward systems, motivation, and power relay mechanisms adopted by the board to ensure the loyalty of employees and maximize the value of the organization.

He can also supervise the preparation of periodic financial and non-financial reports on the results of the entity's business, evaluate its performance, as well as the governance report, and review all responses to the auditors' inquiries before preparing these reports. work in all departments and divisions, follow up the performance of all activities, and take whatever decisions he deems appropriate for the regularity of work and the achievement of goals, as well as work to increase customer satisfaction.

Role and responsibilities of the Secretary of the Board of Directors

The position of the secretary of the Board of Directors is one of the vital and influential positions in the organization, where the entity may form an organizational unit for the secretariat, and the role of the secretary is not limited to recording the minutes of meetings only, but rather it is the link between the members of the board to each other and between them and the management of the entity, and it is also considered an important source for providing the required information, and the necessary powers are granted to him by the Board of Directors.

Governance and the role of state governments and legislative and oversight institutions

Among the tasks and responsibilities of the secretary is to provide the necessary information about the entity to the new members appointed to the board, to coordinate with all board committees to ensure effective communication between those committees and the Board of Directors, to assist the chairman of the board in preparing the meetings of the general assembly of shareholders and to manage their logistics, and to follow up on the issuance and implementation of board decisions.

The secretary informs the concerned departments, as well as prepares follow-up reports on what has been done in their regard, and his tasks go beyond memorizing and documenting everything related to the decisions of the board and the topics presented to him while making sure that the board obtains important information promptly.

Also, adopting the dissemination of the understanding of the principles of governance among the members of the Board of Directors, senior leaders, and all employees of the entity, in a manner that does not conflict with the role of other concerned departments, and coordinating with the concerned committees within the framework of providing the necessary information to support the chairman of the board in the process of evaluating members of the board and members of committees, and the proposals submitted by the board to the general assembly in connection with the selection or replacement of members.

The secretary also contributes to the preparation, preparation, and management of the logistics of the meetings of the board and the various committees, assisting the chairman of the board in preparing the agenda for the meetings, preparing information, data, and details on these

Corporate Governance

topics and sending them to the members in advance, and working to ensure that the members of the board are aware of the most important developments of his supervisory or legal responsibilities as a result of developments in the entity's activities, or in the legal framework to which it is subject, within the limits of his responsibilities and without conflict with the role of the departments concerned with these issues.

CHAPTER SEVEN ...
COMMITTEES EMANATING FROM THE BOARD OF DIRECTORS

The Board of Directors in the economic entity has the authority to form committees of its independent and non-executive members, and by international governance standards, it is preferable that among the members of the committees not be an executive member from the Board of Directors, and each committee is formed of several not less than three members, and some committees with specializations may be merged converging in one committee, without violating the laws and supervisory instructions regulating the work of the board committees.

Controls and determinants of the work of the committees emanating from the Board of Directors

Any committee may seek the help of external consultants to assist it in performing its tasks at the expense of the entity, taking into account obtaining the approval of the Board of Directors in advance and avoiding a conflict of interest.

The entity's annual report must include a brief presentation on the formation of each committee and the number of its meetings during the year and chiefs of the committees must attend the meetings of the organization's

Corporate Governance

general assembly and the committees must also be formed by the work regulations approved by the Board of Directors, which include defining the tasks of each committee, the duration of its work, and the powers granted to it during this period, how the board supervises it and its financial matters.

The committees shall present their reports and recommendations to the Board of Directors to take the necessary decisions, bearing in mind that the committees do not take decisions on behalf of the board, but their role is limited only to submitting recommendations to the board to take the appropriate decisions in their regard.

The committees meet at least once every three months, and the meeting of the committee becomes valid with the presence of half of the number of the committee members or the minimum number of its composition which is 3 members.

Decisions are taken based on the recommendations submitted to the board by the majority of the votes of the members present, and in the event of an equality of votes, the side that includes the chief of the committee is the one preferred.

Each committee must inform the board of its findings, conclusions, or recommendations it makes, and for this to be done with absolute transparency, the board must follow up on the work of the committees periodically to verify that they are carrying out the tasks assigned to them, as the committees are not a means for the board to disavow rather, it is responsible for the performance of those committees and the performance of the entity as a whole.

Committees emanating from the Board of Directors

Formation of the audit committee

The audit committee is formed of independent and non-executive board members, or from outside the entity, provided that at least one member among them has the knowledge and awareness of financial and accounting matters, those that define the scope of their work, responsibilities, and specializations in line with the laws and regulatory instructions workable in the entity.

To achieve the independence of the audit committee, the committee selects its chief, its formation, criteria for selecting its members, its work program, the financial remuneration for its members and its chief, and assigning him to perform his duties according to a decision issued by the Board of Directors.

One of the tasks of the audit committee is to study the financial statements before presenting them to the Board of Directors and to express their opinion and recommendations regarding them, to study the accounting policies used and to express their opinion and recommendations regarding them, and to recommend to the Board of Directors the appointment of one or more auditors, and to verify their qualifications, competence, and independence, and the decision to appoint and determine his fees which will be within the competence of the entity's ordinary general assembly.

The audit committee shall study the auditor's observations and recommendations on the financial statements and others contained in the management letter received from the auditor and follow up on what has been done in their regard, review the auditor's audit plan, and

Corporate Governance

make its observations on it, and recommend approval for the auditor to carry out additional operations other than auditing, and recommend approval on what he receives for those operations in proportion to his annual fees, and to invite the auditor, or the head of the internal audit department, or whoever from inside or outside the entity, to attend its meetings whenever the need arises.

The committee studies and evaluates the entity's early warning system, propose what is necessary to improve it and implement it effectively, studies and evaluates information and data of security systems and how to protect them from any internal or external intrusions, studies observations or violations received from the regulatory authorities and follows up on what has been done in their regard, and implements and follows up any other work assigned to it by the Board of Directors.

The committee shall ensure that the entity is committed to following the internal and external systems, regulations, and laws according to the reports submitted to it by the concerned departments, study the internal control system, prepare a written report on its opinion and recommendations regarding it, discuss and approve the annual plan of the internal audit department, follow up on its efficiency and ensure its comprehensiveness, and review reports of Internal audit, identifying aspects and causes of deficiencies in the entity and following up on corrective actions for these deficiencies.

Committees emanating from the Board of Directors

Formation of the Nominations Committee and the nature of its functions

The Nominations Committee is formed by the Board of Directors from independent and non-executive members, provided that its chief enjoys independence, and among its tasks is to determine the responsibilities of the executive, non-executive and independent members of the board, to develop job descriptions for the senior executive leadership of the organization, to continuously verify the independence of the independent members of the board, and to ensure that the absence of any conflict of interest if the member is a member of the Board of Directors of another organization, and one of its tasks is to carry out the periodic and continuous review of the required requirements of appropriate skills for board membership, and senior management positions, and to prepare a statement of the required qualifications in light of the implementation of the power succession plan.

Formation of the remuneration committee and the nature of its functions

The Remuneration Committee is formed from independent and non-executive board members, taking into account the non-discrimination between what they receive in exchange for the executive members of the board except in the narrowest limits, and this comes while based on specific tasks assigned to them or the committees in which they participate in membership, and this committee has to prepare the annual report detailing all remunerations, privileges, and benefits received by members of the board and senior management for presentation to the general assembly.

This committee also proposes clear policies for the remuneration and entitlements of the members of the Board of Directors, members of committees, and senior executives of the entity, uses performance-related criteria to determine those entitlements, and reviews these policies annually after conducting the necessary studies about remuneration.

This committee shall formulate and prepare a policy for recovering the remuneration and entitlements of the members of the Board of Directors, members of the committees, and senior executives of the entity, if they commit any violations or embezzlement of the capabilities of this entity about the incentive shares, and follow up on that, taking into account that these shares are not an incentive to take decisions that verify the interest of the entity is in the short term only, but it must also be linked to what developed in the performance of the entity in the long term.

Formation of the Risk Management Committee and the nature of its functions

This committee is formed of independent and non-executive members of the Board of Directors, the managing director or the director of risk management in the entity, or any of the executive directors, who can be invited to attend its meetings whenever needed.

This committee also works to assist the Board of Directors in determining and assessing the level of risks that can be accepted, ensuring that the entity does not exceed

Committees emanating from the Board of Directors

this limit of risk, and formulating and preparing the executive frameworks, procedures, and rules adopted by the board to deal with all kinds of risks that the entity may face, which would affect its activity and its sustainability.

The Risk Management Committee supervises and verifies the effectiveness of risk management in the entity in carrying out the work assigned to it, and ensures that it performs its work completely and within the limits of its mandate, as well as ensuring the independence of the risk management staff from the executive management of the organization.

The committee also has to prepare a periodic report on the results of its work and recommendations for presentation to the Board of Directors to take the necessary action.

Formation of the Governance Committee and the nature of its functions

The Governance Committee is formed of independent and non-executive board members. It is concerned with the periodic evaluation of the entity's governance system, drafting internal guides, charters, and policies on how to implement the rules of governance, reviewing the organization's annual report and the board's report, especially about disclosure items and other items related to governance, preserving, documenting, and following up on reports on evaluating the board's performance. Also, one of the tasks entrusted to this committee is to study the observations of the supervisory authorities on the application of governance in the entity, consider that, follow up on what has been done in this matter, and prepare an annual report on the extent of the entity's commitment to the rules of governance, while developing appropriate procedures to complete the application of those rules.

Other committees emanating from the Board of Directors

The Board of Directors in the organization has the power to form other committees that are assigned specific matters according to the need and the nature of the entity's work.

It is the responsibility of the Board of Directors to determine the term of office and powers of these committees, their formation, their financial matters, and the organization of how they work. These committees include the Executive Committee, the Investment Committee, the Social Responsibility Committee, the Environment Protection Committee, the Occupational Safety Committee, and the Policyholders Protection Committee.

Formation of the Executive Committee and the nature of its functions

This committee is usually formed in financial institutions, and there is no objection to its formation in all types of other entities, according to the need for it, and it consists of members of the Executive Board, and it is chaired by the Managing Director, or the CEO, and this committee is responsible for completing the daily business of the entity, Board of Directors monitors and evaluates its performance periodically to ensure its effectiveness.

Committees emanating from the Board of Directors

Formation of the Social Responsibility Committee and the nature of its functions

This committee submits its recommendations to the Board of Directors regarding ways to adhere to social responsibility towards the community and the environment in which the entity operates, ensuring its long-term sustainability and increasing its connection to the community in which it operates.

Formation of the Investment Committee and the nature of its functions

It is a committee that is usually formed in financial institutions, and it may be formed in all types of economic entities according to the need for it, and it consists of members of the Board of Directors and members of senior management, such as the chief executive officer, the investment manager, the financing manager, or the actuaries (the ones who speculate In the entity), to assist the board towards identifying and investing revenues and savings, or customers in investments that generate the best return by the investment policy approved by the Board of Directors, and fulfilling its short and long-term obligations.

Formation of the Occupational Safety and Health Committee and the nature of its functions

This committee is usually formed in industrial organizations, as it becomes concerned with monitoring and following up on the implementation of recommendations related to occupational safety and health for workers in the organization's factories and field sites.

Formation of the Policyholder's Protection Committee and the nature of its functions

This type of committee is usually formed in insurance organizations, to establish appropriate procedures and effective mechanisms to address complaints and grievances of policyholders and to review them periodically, as well as to ensure compliance with the legal requirements stipulated in the regulatory and legal framework through which the relevant entity operates, as well as ensuring the adequacy of required disclosures of material information of interest to policyholders.

Formation of the Environmental Protection Committee and the nature of its functions

This committee is responsible for the environmental policies that must be followed by the entity within the framework of preserving the environment.

CHAPTER EIGHT...
ELEMENTS OF THE CONTROL ENVIRONMENT IN ECONOMIC ENTITIES

What is meant by the control environment in economic entities refers to everything that takes place in the internal work environment of events, as well as the external work environment related to it, which needs to activate all the control tools on them to achieve the discipline required for business, and to preserve all the material and immaterial components of the entity, and these elements it includes the internal control system, the internal audit department, the risk department, the compliance department, the governance department, and the auditor.

The internal control system and its functions

The internal control system is a set of policies, procedures, manuals, and regulations that are prepared by the concerned departments of the economic entity, and approved by the Board of Directors. In addition, this system defines the terms of reference, and complete separation between responsibilities and tasks within the organizational structure of the entity, to provide the discipline required for daily work wheel, and the preservation of the organization's assets.

Corporate Governance

Also among the tasks of this system are achieving complete separation between the responsibilities and powers of all employees of the economic entity, increasing production efficiency, achieving its goals at the lowest costs and with the same quality, and ensuring the accuracy of the implementation of instructions, to make sure that all instructions have been implemented as they should, and ensuring the application of governance rules, this is done through the accurate implementation of its various instructions and rules, ensuring the accuracy and quality of information, so that it provides the entity or others with correct and accurate information about it, protecting the physical assets of the entity from the dangers that it may be exposed to, and register these assets in its records.

Internal Audit Department and its functions

An internal audit is an approach aimed at evaluating the means and systems of internal control in organizations, in addition to establishing a system for predicting and managing risks and ensuring the sound application of governance rules in all departments and executive, financial and legal activities, which ultimately leads to improving performance and achieving the objectives of the entity.

The establishment of the internal audit system and procedures for the entity is based on the perception and study of the risks that may face this entity, and the opinions and reports of the Board of Directors, auditors, and managers of the entity are used in this, and those risks must be updated, monitored and evaluated periodically.

Elements of the control environment in economic entities

Determinants for appointing the director of the internal audit department in economic entities

This type of manager takes charge of the internal audit department, and one of them is chosen from its administrative leaders, and his technical subordination is linked to the audit committee, and he reports administratively to the managing director or CEO of the organization, and the director of the internal audit department must have all the necessary powers, and the audit department must be provided the necessary means, tools, and equipment to carry out its work with the required efficiency.

The Audit Committee defines the objectives, tasks, and powers of the Internal Audit Department, and this is submitted to the Board of Directors of the entity for approval. The director of the Internal Audit Department submits at least a quarterly report to the Audit Committee explaining the results of his work.

The economic entity must support the independence of the internal auditors by providing channels of direct communication with the board and its committees, and ensuring that the employees of the Internal Audit Department obtain important reports and information related to the entity's sectors easily and smoothly, from the Audit Committee, and the Managing Director issues a decision in this regard, and it is not permissible to change his financial treatment or any other benefits he obtains without referring to the Audit Committee.

Corporate Governance

The tasks of the internal audit department in economic entities

Among these tasks are evaluating the efficiency of procedures and policies established and their compatibility with business developments and what is happening in the market, evaluating the efficiency of the entity's internal control system, reporting to the Audit Committee the observations reached, and correcting the observations received in internal and external audit reports and others received from the regulatory authorities, follow-up on that.

The department also has to evaluate the extent to which all departments of the economic entity are committed to carrying out their work by labor procedures and established policies without conflicting with the terms of reference of other concerned departments.

Administration of risk management in the economic entities and their functions

Risk management in the economic entity works on developing strategies related to forecasting, managing risks, and determining the level of risk acceptable to the entity.

This department reports directly to the Board of Directors, and to avoid any conflict of interest, the principle of separation of duties and responsibilities must be applied among the workers in this department, while ensuring that the risk management has direct contact with the board, the risk committee, or the audit committee in the absence of a risk committee so that the risk management submits its

Elements of the control environment in economic entities

periodic reports according to the relative importance of the information it has reached.

One of the tasks and duties of this department is to analyze the risks that the entity may be exposed to, and this analysis must be carried out accurately, at an appropriate and early time, and work to provide accurate and expressive reports so that those concerned can take appropriate decisions in this regard.

This department must also develop a policy for predicting and managing risks, which includes specific indicators for measuring, following up, and controlling the risks that the entity may be exposed to, and determining the level of risk that the entity can accept from the size of the various risks that it may face depending on the impact of these risks, and the extent to which they can be realized.

It must also calculate the extent to which policies are appropriate and effective in terms of measuring, monitoring, and controlling risks, and make any required adjustments in this regard by market developments and the environment surrounding the entity internally and externally while ensuring the availability of appropriate and effective information and communication systems about the process of monitoring and following risks so that it allows senior management, the Risk Committee receives periodic reports from the Risk Management Department that reflect the extent of the entity's commitment to the set risk limits, and clarify the violations of these limits, their reasons, and the proposed plan to address them.

Corporate Governance

Compliance Department and its tasks

The Compliance Department is one of the departments in the economic entity that works to determine the time for providing and evaluating advice, monitoring, and preparing reports related to the risks of non-compliance with laws, regulations, and supervisory instructions issued by various authorities, in an attempt to avoid damage that may be caused to the entity or expose it to resulting penalties for non-compliance, therefore, the responsibility for compliance does not fall on the entity's compliance department only but extends to all its employees.

The responsibility for formulating and setting policies related to the tasks of compliance management rests with the senior management, as the Board of Directors of the entity plays its role in approving these policies and making sure that all employees are informed of these policies, with the knowledge that whoever performs the compliance task administratively reports to the managing director, CEO, or chairman, so the Board of Directors shall submit the reports it prepares to the Audit Committee. Among the tasks entrusted to the Compliance Department is to confirm the existence and review of the plan for updating the data of the entity's employees, and to ensure the follow-up of the extent to which all employees comply with internal regulations, policies, and charters, including the code of ethics and professional conduct that is formulated by the entity, and permanent follow-up and confirmation of the commitment of all personnel activating all binding laws, controls, and supervisory instructions issued by various entities, including governance systems and policies.

Elements of the control environment in economic entities

Finally, confirming that there are no illegal or immoral practices in the entity, including money laundering practices, corruption, and terrorist financing, receiving reports and investigating them objectively and confidentially, presenting them to the review committee, and following up on what has been done in their regard while ensuring the protection of whistleblowers.

Governance department in organizations and its tasks

The Governance Department is one of the departments in the economic entity that works to establish and consolidate the principles of governance, follow up on the application of its principles, and increase its effectiveness, knowing that it reports to the Managing Director, the Chief Executive Officer, or the Chairman of the Board of Directors administratively and technically in terms of preparing and submitting reports to the Governance Committee or the Board of Directors. This department is entrusted with working on clarifying the relations between the Board of Directors and the stakeholders, monitoring the application of the policy of avoiding conflict of interests to all employees, working on applying the concept of transparency, clarity, and fairness in dealing with all shareholders and monitoring the application of the principle of disclosure, transparency, and the culture of governance in all sectors, business, and activities of the economic entity.

Among its tasks is to monitor the availability of basic principles and elements that help develop and improve the entity's performance in a way that contributes to achieving the strategic objectives set by the Board of Directors, and to

Corporate Governance

improve and develop the general framework and principles of the entity's work through the entity's professional code of conduct, while defining its social responsibility and towards workers and society as a whole, working on formulating various internal policies that regulate the relationship between all workers, developing internal governance evidence for the entity, as well as contributing to preparing reports on the extent of the economic entity's commitment to governance.

The entity's auditor, contracting determinants and tasks

The General Assembly shall, upon a nomination by the Board of Directors and after a recommendation by the Audit Committee, contract with one or more auditors for the entity. The decision to appoint him and estimate his fees shall be within the competence of the Ordinary General Assembly provided that he/they fulfill the conditions stipulated in the Law of Practicing the Accounting and Auditing Profession, including competence, reputation, and sufficient experience, and that his capabilities are commensurate with the size and nature of the activity of the economic entity, and the stakeholders he deals with.

The auditor is not contracted as a natural person for more than five years, and should not be re-contracted before the expiry of three years from the date of termination of his work as the entity's auditor. It is preferable for large economic entities to appoint two auditors to manage their accounts.

The auditor must attach a copy of his report with the report prepared by the entity on the extent of its

Elements of the control environment in economic entities

commitment to the principles of governance to the administrative body by the governance rules and disclosure in force. A copy of this report shall also be submitted to the General Assembly of Shareholders. The Board of Directors may not contract an auditor to perform any additional job unrelated to his work as an auditor of the entity's accounts, directly or indirectly, except after obtaining the approval of the Audit Committee, and provided that this overtime work is prohibited for the auditor to do it.

The fees for performing the additional work must also be commensurate with the nature and size of the required work. The Audit Committee, when considering the approval of the auditor's performance of the additional work and determining his fees, to take into account that this does not affect his independence, with the need to disclose this in the general assembly of shareholders and the annual report.

The auditor must be completely independent of the economic entity and from the members of its Board of Directors. It is not allowed to be a shareholder in it or a member of its Board of Directors, be related to any of the members of its Board of Directors or senior management up to the second degree, or to be a permanent any technical, administrative or consulting work in it, and he must be impartial in what he expresses of opinions, and his work must also be immune from the interference of the Board of Directors.

CHAPTER NINE ...
THE GENERAL ASSEMBLY OF SHAREHOLDERS IN ECONOMIC ENTITIES

The General Assembly is composed of all the shareholders of the economic entity, each according to the percentage of the shares he owns, and the basic system of the entity may stipulate that only the shareholder who owns a certain number of shares may attend the meeting, this is an exception to the rule that gives every shareholder the right to attend the General Assembly, and it is only resorted to when the number of shareholders exceeds the ability of the entity to manage the venue for the meeting, bearing in mind that this right may not be used as a means to ignore the shareholders who own the small number of shares.

The date and place of the meeting of the General Assembly shall be arranged for the shareholders in a way that facilitates their attendance while adhering to the law and the articles of association of the economic entity about the procedures for calling the General Assembly and how to manage them. In the case of entities to which large numbers of shareholders are affiliated, according to the best international standards, these entities can use modern electronic means and various communication systems to provide an opportunity to transmit or record the proceedings of the meeting to shareholders abroad or at home.

The general assembly of shareholders in economic entities

Determinants of the course of the meetings of the general assembly of shareholders

Each subject must be presented for discussion within the agenda of the Ordinary or Extraordinary General Assembly, accompanied by all data and information that enable sound and thoughtful decision-making. All inquiries from shareholders, whether sent before the meeting, must be answered to be included in the agenda or to allocate sufficient time during the meeting to respond to those inquiries.

Through the meetings of the General Assembly, shareholders are allowed to express their opinions in the light of what is regulated by the law and the articles of association and by the agenda of the assembly, and the management of the entity must fully and sufficiently disclose all topics included in the agenda of the assembly. A secretary is appointed for the General Assembly, and the persons entrusted with counting the votes of referendums on the listed topics are appointed, other than the members of the General Assembly and the Board of Directors of the economic entity.

To obtain reliable results of referendums related to the topics on the agenda of the General Assembly meetings, and so that the final results reflect the proportional representation of all shareholders, it is preferable to use the "cumulative voting" method, provided that this is stipulated in the entity's articles of association, to represent all shareholders shares when electing members of the Board of Directors to know that a brief biography of each candidate for membership of the entity's Board of Directors must be

Corporate Governance

submitted to the shareholders when inviting them to elect the Board.

Voting on the decisions of the General Assembly of the economic entity is recorded with extreme accuracy and in the event of any dispute arising regarding the validity of some votes on all or some of the decisions presented to the General Assembly, voting is taken into consideration the validity of these votes once and their invalidity again to be presented later to the competent administrative or judicial authority so that the procedures of the General Assembly continue, and by the laws in force and the articles of association of each entity, minority shareholders who own at least 5% of the issued capital of the entity are entitled to request to add items to the agenda of the General Assembly>

As well as objecting to the decisions of the General Assembly of the administrative body, as it, in turn, suspends the decisions of the General Assembly that are issued in favor of the majority group of shareholders against the minority group of them, and that 3% or more of the shareholders have the right to oblige the entity to hold a General Assembly meeting in the form regulated by law To protect the rights of minority shareholders.

The secretary of the association drafts the minutes of the meeting of the General Assembly so that it includes all the discussions, events, and decisions that took place at the meeting, and the entity discloses the decisions that were taken, and all the essential events to all at the same time.

The entity must publish the minutes of the meeting of its General Assembly on its website, in addition, to making it available in print to the public whenever possible, and the entity registered in the stock exchange must be committed

The general assembly of shareholders in economic entities

to providing the market with the decisions of the ordinary and extraordinary General Assembly immediately upon its completion, and at a maximum before the start of the first trading session following the end of the meeting, to achieve the correct availability of information for all.

The Board of Directors of the economic entity must obtain the prior approval of the General Assembly of shareholders about all transactions with groups related to the entity, related parties, and netting contracts that are under the procedure, to avoid the occurrence of conflicts of interest, especially with major shareholders, or members of the Board of Directors, or any other related entities, with the knowledge that the party involved in the netting contract is not entitled to vote in the General Assembly, with an emphasis on not harming the interest of the entity and other stakeholders, and the necessity of full disclosure of the netting contracts offered for the following year, or what was done regarding the netting contracts concluded in the previous year.

CHAPTER TEN ...
RULES AND METHODS OF APPLYING GOVERNANCE IN ECONOMIC ENTITIES

The availability of information in various economic entities, such as organizations, business establishments, and companies, plays an important role in decision-making, performance evaluation, and recognition of the entity's climate in its internal and external environment alike, therefore measuring the extent of transparency and disclosure of financial and non-financial matters is the decisive factor in applying good governance.

A good rational governance based on honest transparency, and disclosure that follows a policy of complete clarity and shows all facts, financial and non-financial information, and material events about the entity that is of interest to investors, related parties, and also all society parties, must have a significant impact on the efficiency, credibility, and market balance, justice and protection for investors and stakeholders, which supports the investment climate and the economy as a whole.

Managing the principles of transparency and disclosure in economic entities requires great skill, wisdom, and tact from decision-makers, as it requires presenting this promptly and in a manner that prevails in justice, and is accessible to all relevant parties so that they can make and implement appropriate decisions based on correct and accurate information. The transparency of positions provides a climate that allows all the required information or data.

For both transparency and disclosure to bear fruit, the information that is disclosed must be credible, measurable, comparable, and documented, and it must be published periodically and characterized by clarity, and the essential events about their occurrence.

Financial and other non-financial information that must be included in the disclosure principle

The economic entity must disclose, by adopting various means, the entity's financial and other non-financial information, which is primarily of interest to shareholders and stakeholders, such as dividend distributions, reports of boards of directors, accounting policies, estimated budgets, asset evaluation methods, and annual financial statements, and periodic auditor reports.

The entity must also disclose non-financial information and data, such as the ownership structure of the entity, including the main shareholders and owners of influential stakes, provided that it shows the owners who benefit directly and indirectly from those stakes, as well as the ownership structures of sister entities affiliated with the main entity, and transactions with related parties and netting contracts, which are matters of concern to shareholders, current and prospective investors.

Corporate Governance

The entity must also disclose internal information that includes the objectives and vision of this entity, the nature of its activity, its plans, its future strategy, the composition of the Board of Directors and its committees, who they are and its senior executives, and introduce the administrative competencies of the entity, the biography of each of them as well as the systems for raising competencies, training, and rewards, care for the employees of this entity, and the remuneration and allowances received by members of the Board of Directors, its committees, and senior executives during the year.

The matter does not stop at this point, but the economic entity must work to disclose the most important risks that it may face, ways to confront them, and the possibility of changing the approved investment policy, in addition to deciding the extent to which the entity adheres to the rules of governance, to achieve the best possible rates of sustainability in the long term.

In addition to the aforementioned information that must be disclosed, the economic entity must also disclose the essential external information that affects it and prepare correct comparisons on this information, those that may affect business continuity, such as the availability of natural resources, raw materials, and the source of the energy on which the entity relies, and the ability to deal with any fluctuations in these matters.

Likewise, the entity must disclose to its shareholders and the supervisory authorities about the treasury shares, and if the subsidiary entity purchases the shares of the holding entity that owns it, all the rules of treasury shares apply to the purchased shares, and they are not counted in the quorum of shareholders and do not participate in voting on the decisions of the General Assembly.

Investor relations department function

The so-called investor relations management function is in itself an independent strategy aimed at revitalizing and consolidating the relationship of the economic entity with current and prospective investors, as it works to open channels of communication with those related to the capital and investment market, and also works to provide the necessary principles of disclosure and transparency. which makes it one of the main departments for applying the principles of governance in economic entities.

Among the positive effects obtained from this function of this department is to work to achieve appropriate liquidity for trading the entity's shares in the stock market, and to provide a field of vision for investors to know the current performance of the entity, and their expectations for its future performance, and work to reduce the cost of financing in the long term, and increase the confidence of dealers with the entity, and with stakeholders, as well as promoting an increase in groups supporting the entity.

The Investor Relations Department reports to the Chairman of the Board of Directors or the Managing Director of the economic entity, and it must submit its periodic reports to them. The entity must understand and support this management to be an effective communication tool with each of the shareholders, stakeholders, and dealers with the entity, to ensure that they get their share of the attention and follow-up of the market.

Accordingly, the Investor Relations Department is one of the effective means that enables the Board of Directors to understand the reasons for the performance of the shares of the economic entity, and its reflection on its fair value according to the information provided by the entity about its performance, capabilities, and future, and the extent to which the entity adheres to the rules of disclosure, communication with investors, and the clarity of their vision and the evaluation of the investment in the market for them.

Duties of the investor relations officer in the economic entity

One of the most important tasks of the investor relations officer in the existing economic entities is to participate in formulating and developing a strategy for communicating with investment markets, opening channels of communication with investors, and conveying market views and investor concerns to the Board of Directors on an ongoing basis.

In general, the investor relations officer must attend the meetings of the General Assembly of the entity, and he can also be invited to attend the meetings of the Board of Directors to get acquainted with internal matters and its strategic directions. He must also organize meetings and visits for current and prospective investors to let them get to know the entity, and its senior management, details of its activities, and level of performance.

Rules and methods of applying governance
in economic entities

The investor relations officer must have full knowledge of the economic entity, its financial position and be able to respond to investors' questions and inquiries and know the decisions that have an impact on business results, as well as know what can be disclosed, and what is not authorized to be disclosed through its application of the rules regulating disclosure and transparency in the market.

In sum, we can collect the vocabulary of the tasks entrusted to the investor relations officer in the following points:

• The most important thing that can be done is to make every effort to preserve existing investors and attract new ones by educating the market about the business of the economic entity, the future growth opportunities available for this entity, and identifying the factors that affect its profitability.

• Work on formulating and developing a strategy for Investor Relations Department programs by understanding the market and the entity's requirements, defining priorities about the required activities, formulating and developing the strategy required to implement these activities in cooperation with the Board of Directors, and introducing the market to new members of the Board of Directors or Senior Management.

• Organizing the information issued by the entity by the rules and disclosure policy approved by the Board of Directors, which he participated in drafting, preparing the required disclosure reports from the economic entity, preparing pages for the Investor Relations Department on the entity's website, and working to update them continuously.

- Communicating with investors through various communication tools, such as the economic entity's website, social networking sites, and press reports, and participating in preparing the annual report that current and prospective investors are interested in, organizing promotional campaigns and events on the entity, facilitating investors' visits to the various economic entity sites, and working to create a database of investors, whether in terms of the type of investor or its geographical location and follow them up constantly to update their data and identify their activities.

- Communicating with analysts, investors, and media representatives, and providing information to reduce the rumors, and the occurrence of surprises that may lead to fluctuations in the prices and stop trading the shares of the economic entity.

Disclosure tools and methods that can be used

First: The disclosure report issued by the economic entity

This report must be issued every three months in the year, i.e., it is a quarterly report prepared by the entity's management with the participation of its Investor Relations Department, and it includes the following data:

- A report on the entity's treasury shares details.

- A report on the total shareholder structure, showing the free float shares.

- Statement of the formation of committees emanating from the Board of Directors.

Rules and methods of applying governance in economic entities

• Statement of changes in the company's Board of Directors and the last formation of the board.

• A report on the structure of shareholders who own 5% or more of the shares of the economic entity.

• Data on the names of the investor relations officials and their contact details, and contact details for the entity.

Second: The annual report of the economic entity

The economic entity is obligated to issue an annual report that includes a summary of the Board of Directors' report, and the financial statements, in addition to all other information of interest to shareholders, current investors, prospective others, and stakeholders. The language of this annual report should be clear and easy. All parties are to view it, regardless of their nationalities.

This annual report is one of the most important sources of information about the economic entity, its activity, and its financial position for the current and prospective investor. It is considered a report from the entity's management for all those interested in knowing what happened in the past year, and what the entity aims to achieve during the coming year. This report must contain:

• Corporate Governance Report.

• Statement of vision and purpose.

• A statement on the entity's strategy.

• Speech of the Chairman or Managing Director.

Corporate Governance

- A report on the entity's current and future projects.

- A statement on the ownership structure of the entity.

- Statement of analysis of the financial position of the entity.

- A statement of the market analysis in which the entity is located.

- A report on the social and environmental responsibility of the entity.

- A report on the executive management's discussion of the entity's financial performance.

- A report on the history of the entity and the most important stations it went through.

- The auditor's report and the comparative financial statements for the same previous periods.

- A statement of the members of the Senior Management and the composition of the Board of Directors.

Third: The report of the Board of Directors of the economic entity

The economic entity must issue an annual report for presentation to the General Assembly and the regulatory authorities. It shall be addressed by the Chairman of the Board to the shareholders, and it shall include the following points:

Rules and methods of applying governance in economic entities

- A statement on the strategy approved by the economic entity.

- Reports related to previous and subsequent netting contracts.

- Statement of the main achievements of the entity during the past year.

- A report on the policies of rewarding and motivating the entity's employees.

- Statement of major changes in the structure of the administrative entity.

- A report on the financial results and material issues of the entity.

- Report on the application of governance and social and environmental responsibility.

- Statement of the composition of the Board of Directors and the number of times it convenes.

- A statement on the analysis related to the entity's main business environment and markets.

- Statement of the formation of the board committees and the number of times they are convened.

- A report on the actions taken against the entity, or any of its board members or managers, by the supervisory or judicial authorities.

- A report on the average number of employees in the entity during the year and the average income of the employee during the same period.

Fourth: Governance report in the economic entity

This report shows the extent to which the relevant economic entity is committed to applying the rules of governance, as well as what may be justifications for non-compliance with some of these applications according to the rule of compliance or interpretation. This report must include:

- A report on relations with shareholders.

- A statement of power relay planning in the entity.

- A statement of the formation of board committees.

- A statement of the number of meetings of the board.

- A statement on the formation of the Board of Directors of the entity.

- A report on all significant information related to governance.

- A statement of the plan set to complete the governance applications.

- A report on the internal dealings of the entity's stockholders.

- A statement on the organizational structure of the economic entity.

Rules and methods of applying governance in economic entities

- A statement of evaluation of the internal control system and compliance.

- A statement of compliance with the entity's approved disclosure rules.

- A statement that includes the introduction and procedures for implementing governance.

- A report on the evaluation of the performance of the board and the executive management.

- A report on the actions taken against the entity, or any of its board members or managers, by the supervisory or judicial authorities.

Fifth: Sustainability report in the economic entity

The economic entity must issue a balanced report on sustainability, containing the achievements in the economic, environmental, and social fields. This report presents the values and principles of the economic entity and clarifies the relationship between its strategy and its obligations towards the society in which it operates.

When preparing this report, the entity must take into account ensuring transparency, accuracy, completeness, comprehensiveness, and impartiality, that the data and numbers contained in the report are comparable, and that the information contained therein is appropriate to the needs of stakeholders, and that it is available at regular times that allow for the provision of information promptly, suitable for entity employees to assist them in decision-making.

Corporate Governance

This report must also work to achieve the principle of disclosing sustainability towards a set of benefits represented in supporting the reputation of the entity, continuous improvement in performance, compliance with legislation and regulatory instructions in the environmental and social fields, as well as how to manage the risks that the economic entity may be exposed to, as well as ways to motivate its employees and attract capital.

The sustainability report should include the following topics:

- A report on anti-fraud and corruption policies.

- A report on the social and environmental responsibility policy of the economic entity.

- A report on government relations and political participation of the economic entity.

- A report on ensuring business continuity, risk and crisis management, and information protection.

- A report on the quality of products and services provided by the entity, and the complaints handling system.

- A report on the economic entity's policy towards the environment in which it operates and its impact on it.

- A report on the governance policy and control of the professional behavior of workers in the economic entity.

*Rules and methods of applying governance
in economic entities*

• A report on the economic entity's policy regarding employee relations, human rights, and policies to ensure nondiscrimination.

Sixth: The contents of the economic entity's website

In this era of information and advanced communications, it will be imperative for the economic entity to have a website on the Internet, preferably in more than one language, so that financial and non-financial information can be disclosed through it in a way that is easy for the user, and this website must be updated with information on an ongoing basis, and to provide the ability to communicate through it with the entity in an easy manner, with the obligation to follow up on responding to messages and inquiries that the entity receives through this site.

The website of the economic entity must include:

• Annual reports of the economic entity.

• Governance policy within the economic entity.

• Social responsibility policy of the economic entity.

• How to receive customer suggestions and complaints.

• An overview of the entity, its vision, mission, and strategy.

• Pages dedicated to investor relations and how to contact them directly.

• Information about the entity's activity, products, and scope of work.

Corporate Governance

- Formation of the board of directors, its committees, and senior management.

- Address and contact information for the economic entity and its branches, if any.

- Financial statements and periodic and annual business results compared to previous periods.

CHAPTER ELEVEN ... GOVERNANCE POLICIES AND REGULATIONS IN ECONOMIC ENTITIES

The application of governance in economic entities is governed by each of the policies and regulations to regulate these applications, the policies are divided into what is called *the policy of succession of power, the policy of disclosure, the policy of reporting violations, policies for preventing conflicts of interest, and the policy of social and environmental responsibility by the economic entity*.

As for the regulations, they include *the charter of ethics and professional conduct, the work regulations of the Board of Directors for the economic entity, and the work regulations of the board committees*.

The policy of succession of power in the economic entity

This policy aims to create procedures and evaluate selection, appointment, and promotion processes through a better insurance framework for the qualified elements of the entity in the appropriate locations, and at the same time encourage professional development and advancement of the current employees, and develop a plan for succession of authority at the level of executive management in emergency conditions or the short term, or the long term, with a focus on planning the succession of authority for the main elements through the entity's human resources procedures guide, and preparing a list of candidates to occupy key positions periodically and effectively, to achieve added value to the entity and ensure its sustainability.

This type of policy can include both the objective of the policy, the scope of its application, and its principles that include sustainability and continuity of activity, the application of justice, effectiveness, efficiency, availability of transparency, and objectivity.

Disclosure policy in the economic entity

This policy aims to regulate the process of disclosing information in compliance with the rules of disclosure and transparency, which aim at the need to inform all dealers of the entity of the information of interest and to do so in an equal and fair manner.

This policy includes each of its objectives and fields of application, identifying and defining the financial and non-financial disclosures that must be disclosed periodically other than material events, and defining the means of disclosure approved by the economic entity, such as the website, various periodic reports, press releases, and participation in conferences and other events. ..etc.

This policy also defines the persons who are allowed to disclose, the information that should not be disclosed, and what must be done in case of unintentional disclosure of material information.

Governance policies and regulations in economic entities

Policy for reporting violations in economic entities

This policy aims to encourage employees of the economic entity or those who deal with it to report any practices that violate the rules of ethical behavior or any illegal actions and to call for the application of effective measures concerning the principles of accountability and responsibility.

And then enhance the standards of honesty and integrity in all the various activities of the economic entity, and this policy also protects those who report, to ensure that the entity's employees and others are encouraged to take the initiative to detect and report violations, while ensuring the complete confidentiality of the amount, taking into account that the reporting process must be completed based on objective and credible documents or information.

The purpose of this policy is to name the committee formed to review cases related to ethical behavior, evaluate the risks associated with it, and prepare general directions for stating the policy of reporting violations that include reporting procedures, the confidentiality of information, and the identity of those involved, protection of the whistleblower, and investigation procedures in reported violations.

Also, this policy will resort to some significant expressions such as fraud and embezzlement, channels dedicated to reporting violations, immoral matters…etc.

Corporate Governance

Policy to prevent conflicts of interest in economic entities

This policy is divided into two types of policies. The first policy is called the policy of dealing with insiders, and the second policy is called the policy of dealing with related and associated parties.

Policy of dealing with insiders

It is a policy that governs the process of insider trading on the shares of the entity following the rules of the regulatory authorities and ensures that all concerned parties understand the definition of insider trading and the rules for its organization. ***This policy includes the objective of this policy, and the definition of what is meant by insider trading, insiders, closed period, insider information, material events...etc.***

One of the tasks of this policy is to verify the misuse of insider information and to identify the restrictions placed by the regulatory authorities and the entity on the dealings of insiders.

Policy of dealing with related and associated parties

We must take into account that the dealings of related persons about inter-communication may represent a kind of conflict of interest, so this policy aims to set standards to control the dealings of related persons in a way that does not prejudice the interest of the entity and preserves the rights of its shareholders.

Governance policies and regulations in economic entities

This policy will include achieving its objective, defining the transactions that are subject to this policy, including the term **"related parties"**, defining criteria for approving transactions with related persons, and ways of approving these transactions.

Social and environmental responsibility policy by the economic entity

The economic entity formulates and establishes a clear policy regarding its social and environmental responsibility and its continuous commitment to contribute to economic and societal development. Through this policy, the entity works to clarify the objective of that, define the social responsibility of this entity, and define the scope of its work about this responsibility, especially toward the stakeholders including employees, suppliers, customers, competitors...etc.

Through the application of this policy, the themes of the entity's responsibility towards society, the themes of responsibility towards the environment, and the initiatives in which the entity participates related to both social and environmental responsibility are defined.

Charter of ethics and professional conduct of the economic entity

This Charter includes a set of values that control and regulate the rules of professional behavior and ethics within the economic entity, and it contains standards of behavior that all workers must follow and observe in all transactions, and in every location in which they perform their work, in a way that positively affects the reputation and credibility of the entity, and the integrity of its employees, in a way that guarantees the rights of shareholders and all those who deal with it, and this charter is the subject of commitment by all employees of the relevant economic entity.

Regulations for the work of the board of directors of the economic entity

These regulations refer to the standards that govern the performance of the Board of Directors, and they are binding standards for the Chairman and all of its members. They include defining the role of the Board of Directors, its composition, and its duties, the powers granted to it, and the Board's relationship with shareholders.

These regulations determine the number of Board meetings, the correct quorum for meetings, the responsibilities, and duties of the chairman of the board, the methodology for taking decisions of the board, the issue of avoiding conflicts of interest, the required confidentiality, how to deal with the entity's shares, the methodology for evaluating the performance of the board members and defining the responsibilities of the secretary of the Board of Directors.

Work regulations of the board committees of the economic entity

These are the regulations that govern the work and performance of the formed committees by the Board of Directors, and they are binding on the heads and members of those committees. These regulations include the process

Governance policies and regulations in economic entities

of forming the various committees, defining their responsibilities and tasks, determining the correct quorum for the meetings of these committees, defining their powers and the number of their meetings, and formulating a methodology for preparing the minutes of the committee's meetings, and the methodology and periodicity of the reports presented to the Board of Directors on the results of the work of these committees.

REFERENCES

*- Bilal Amin Zain al-Din - The phenomenon of administrative corruption in the Arab countries and comparative legislation, first edition, Alexandria, 2009.

*- Adel Abdel Aziz Al-Sun - Legal and Economic Aspects of Money Laundering Crimes, Arab Administrative Development Organization, Administrative and Financial Corruption in the Arab World, Sharjah, United Arab Emirates, publications of the Arab Organization for Administrative Development, Cairo, 2007.

*- Ahmed Mohamed Al-Shami, Administrative Corruption in Public Service Units. Its concept, measurement, manifestations, the cost to society, methods of combating it, a working paper presented to the Seventh Conference of Administrative Leaders, held in Sana'a during the period 26-28 November 2007, National Institute of Administrative Sciences, Sana'a, Yemen.

*- Adel bin Ahmed Al-Shalfan, Administrative Corruption in Public Institutions - The Problem and the Solution, Journal of the Faculty of Commerce, Volume 25, Issues One and Two, January and July 2003, Faculty of Commerce, Zagazig University, Egypt.

*- Ahmed Saqr Ashour, Successes and Failures in Anti-Corruption Programs: Lessons Learned from International Experiences, research presented to the New Horizons Conference on Integrity, Transparency and Administrative

Accountability, a Strategic and Institutional Perspective, 1st Edition, Cairo: Publications of the Arab Organization for Administrative Development, 2001.

*- The Financial Regulatory Authority, Egyptian Directors Center, Egyptian Guide to Corporate Governance, Third Edition - 2006.

www.ingramcontent.com/pod-product-compliance
Lightning Source LLC
Chambersburg PA
CBHW071421210526
45465CB00001B/486